Trousers

SIMPLE DRESSMAKING 2

Maureen Goldsworthy

G000230132

Mills & Boon Ltd
London   Sydney   Toronto

I am most grateful to Jill Hilyer and my
daughter Alice Helps, who modelled the
trousers, and to Robert Saunders of Wright
Photography who took the photographs at
Warwick Castle by kind permission of
Warwick Castle Ltd.

For C.C.B.

First published in 1980

© Maureen Goldsworthy 1980

ISBN 0 263 06426 3

Designed by Richard Brown Associates

Printed in Great Britain by
Fletcher & Son Ltd, Norwich
and bound by
Richard Clay (The Chaucer Press) Ltd, Bungay, Suffolk
for the publishers Mills & Boon Ltd,
15–16 Brooks Mews,
London W1Y 1LF

CONTENTS

INTRODUCTION   **4**

MATERIALS NEEDED FOR PATTERN DRAFTING   **5**

PERSONAL MEASUREMENT CHART   **6**

DRAFTING THE BLOCKS   **7**
Drawing curves   Drafting the front block   Drafting the
back block   Transferring the blocks to card

DESIGNING THE PATTERN   **14**
The draft pattern   The leg shape   Turn-ups
The waist level   Yokes   Trousers with body fullness
Pockets   The zip   The waist finish   Seam and hem
allowances   Fabric requirements

MAKING UP THE TROUSERS   **44**
Cutting out   Marking   Fitting   The darts   Yokes
Patch pockets   Patch pockets from side seams   Trouser
side pockets   Side seams   Inside-leg seams
The crutch seam   The zip   The waist finish   Hem finishes

INTRODUCTION

This book contains all the information you need to make well-fitting trousers in any style you wish: widely-flared, narrowly-tapered or full and gathered.

The first section shows how to draft the basic block patterns from your own measurement chart. The next part of the book shows how to translate these blocks into a working pattern for the design you have chosen. The last section gives full instructions for making up the trousers.

The disadvantage of using a commercial pattern – apart from the price – is that it will be in a stock size, designed for average proportions. But individual figures vary widely in the seat measurements, which is why many people find difficulty in achieving a good fit from a bought pattern. By drafting your personal blocks, based on six of your own measurements, you can be sure of an exact, unwrinkled fit at every point. All your future trouser patterns, of whatever style, are derived from the permanent record of the blocks.

None of this is difficult, though to begin with it does take a little time. You will probably need a couple of hours to draft the blocks, then another couple to make the final pattern with all the styling details. But if you can follow an ordinary dressmaking pattern, you should have no trouble with these instructions.

Paper

Squared dressmaker's paper may be difficult to find and is expensive. The plain variety comes in sheets that are too wide for easy handling. It is much better to use a roll of ceiling lining paper. This is strong, easily obtainable and quite wide enough. Besides, you will need plenty of it and it is cheap.

Thin card

This is obtainable from art stationers. Two large sheets will be needed for the final pattern blocks.

Set square

This is handy but not essential. Without one, lines at exact right angles to the edge of the paper can be made by creasing. When you fold across the width of the paper, keep the side edges exactly level with each other; the creases will then be at right angles to the side edges (*Figure 1*). Any tendency for the paper to curl up can be cured by pressing with a cool iron.

Tracing wheel

A wheel with sharp metal points used to transfer pattern outlines from an upper to a lower sheet of paper. Obtainable from haberdashery (US notions) departments (*Figure 2*). A plastic wheel will not do.

Carbon paper

This is for transferring double-thickness markings.

Pencils

Hard pencils (H or 2H). Coloured fibre-tip pens are also useful.

Long ruler or straight edge

Tape measure

This should be marked in centimetres. If you have not yet tried working in centimetres, now is the time to do so. The metric system is actually much easier to use than the imperial system, and you should not attempt to convert one to the other; this is why alternative inch measurements are not given. Just take the centimetres as they come – one soon gets over the shock of one's hip measurement hovering around the hundred mark.

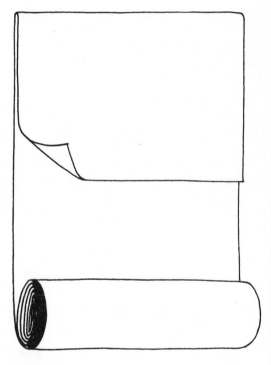

Figure 1

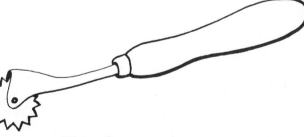

Figure 2

5

PERSONAL MEASUREMENT CHART

Six body measurements are needed for constructing the trouser pattern blocks. You must have the help of a friend to measure you; it is impossible to do this accurately for yourself.

Measurements should be taken closely but not tightly. The extra ease needed for movement in the trousers should not be allowed for as it is built into the block patterns (*Figure 3*).

1 Waist, taken firmly at the natural waistline_____cm
Quarter waist measurement_____cm

2 Hip, taken over the widest part of the hip, usually 20–22 cm below the waist

_____cm

Quarter hip measurement_____cm
One-eighth hip measurement_____cm

3 Hip depth – the measurement from the waist down to the widest part of the hip, taken down the side_____cm

4 Body rise – the measurement that gives the depth of the crotch below the waistline. Sit on a hard chair and measure down the side of the body from the waistline to the seat of the chair_____cm

5 Waist to knee length, taken down the side seam_____cm

6 Finished length, taken down the side seam. Be generous here: trousers, particularly if they are to be flared, may look best if they are cut almost to floor-length_____cm

Figure 3

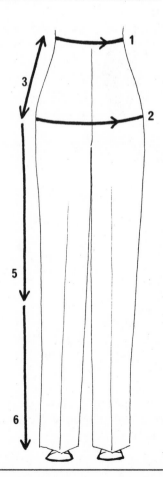

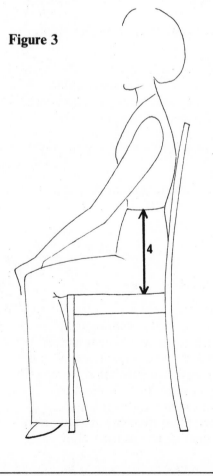

DRAFTING THE BLOCKS

Block patterns are not fashion shapes and contain no styling. Nor do they include seam and hem allowances; so they cannot be used directly as dressmaking patterns. They are simply the essential record of your bone structure, from which the final pattern is built. Even changes in your weight will not substantially affect the fit. A couple of centimetres more, or less, on hip or waist just means that you need to add or subtract a quarter of that amount on the side seam edges of the final pattern – which you can do without cutting a new block. The blocks provide, however, a permanent fit for the important structural measurements – the depth of the pelvis from back to front and the proportion of pelvis to leg length.

The block pattern used in this book is designed to give a very close fit at the waist and round the hips. This is made possible by a rather generous 'through' measurement from front to back, at the crotch level, which allows the trouser back to fall straight from the waistline (as shown by the photograph on page 8), without cutting in under the seat. In front, there should be no pulling across the crotch.

If, however, you like an easier fit at waist and hipline, then alternative measurements are given in the instructions for cutting the back block. With trousers, a very small alteration will make a great deal of difference to the fit.

DRAWING CURVES

Pattern drafting consists mainly of measuring and ruling straight lines, but sometimes you will need to draw a curve to connect three or more points. Here is the simplest way to draw a smooth curve.

Always draw from the inside of the curve, so that the movement of your hand goes naturally with the line, rather than against it. If you draw as shown in *Figure 4*, you will have less control over your pencil and the line may wobble. But turn the paper round, draw as shown in *Figure 5*, and the movement of your hand will then assist the curve.

For a full curve, rest the heel of your hand on the paper and use it as a pivot. For a very shallow curve, use your elbow as a pivot. Draw quickly: the curve will be smoother than if you tense your fingers and go slowly.

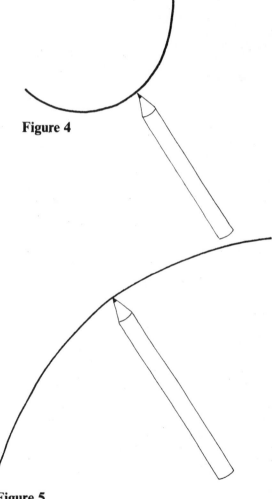

Figure 4

Figure 5

DRAFTING THE FRONT BLOCK

Cut a rectangle of lining paper, making sure that the sides are parallel to each other.

Length – the finished length of the trousers plus 0·5 cm.
Width – quarter hip plus 20 cm.

As in *Figure 6*, crease right down the paper 8 cm from the left-hand edge. Mark A at the top of the crease.

Measuring along the top edge:
A–B is quarter hip;
A–C is one-eighth hip, plus 2 cm.

Measuring down the crease:
A–D is hip depth. Crease right across the paper from D to E for the hipline. D–F is quarter hip.
A–G is body rise. Crease right across the paper from G to H for the crotch level. G–J is quarter hip.
A–K is waist to knee length. Crease right across the paper from K to L for the knee level.

M–N, 0·5 cm up from the bottom edge of the paper, is the same length as A–C.

Crease right down the paper from C to N, to give the line of the trouser front crease. Mark P where this line crosses K–L, and mark Q where it crosses G–H.

To shape the waistline
Mark R, 1 cm down from B.
R–S is quarter waist, plus 2 cm.
Join R–S with a straight line.
Mark T, 10 cm below C.
Mark U and V, 1 cm each side of C.
Join U–T–V for the front dart.

To shape the centre-front seam
Join R–F
J–W is a quarter of the length A–B (i.e. one-sixteenth hip)
Rule a straight line between F and W.
Join F–W with a shallow curve, dropping 1·5 cm inside the straight line.

For the side seam
Rule a straight line between S and D.
Join S–D with a shallow curve, up to 0·5 cm outside the straight line. The rest of the seam, from D to M, is a straight line.

For the inside-leg seam
P–X is the same length as P–K.
N–Y is the same length as N–M.
Rule a straight line between W and X.
Join W–X with a shallow curve, up to 1 cm inside the straight line.
Join X–Y with a straight line.

For the hemline
Mark Z, 0·5 cm above N.
Join M–Z–Y in a shallow curve for the instep shaping.
Mark the whole outline of the front block pattern with a heavy black line, as shown in *Figure 6*.

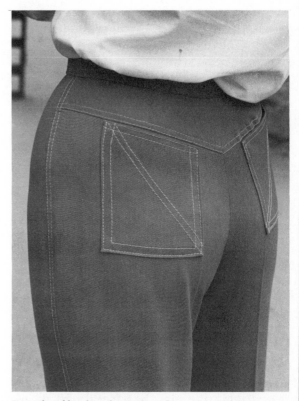

Details of back yoke and pocket top-stitching

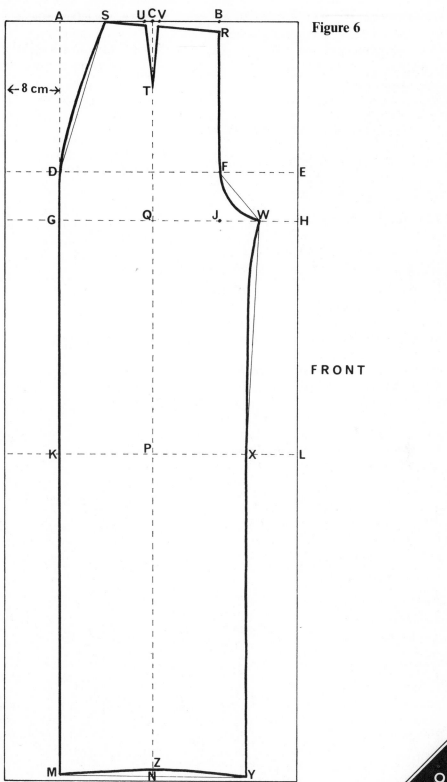

Figure 6

←8 cm→

FRONT

DRAFTING THE BACK BLOCK

Continue on the same pattern paper. *Figure 7*
(The lightly-marked line represents the front
block you have just drawn.)
J–a is half the length of J–W;
W–b is the same length as J–a;
C–c is the same length as Q–a.
Join c–a, and mark d where this line crosses
D–E.
Mark e, 1·5 cm to the left of c.
Mark f, 2 cm above d.
Mark g, 0·5 cm below b.

To shape the centre-back seam

Join e–f.
Rule a straight line between f and g.
Join f–g with a curved line dropping 2 cm
inside the straight line.

To shape the waistline

e–h is quarter waist plus 4 cm (if you like a
close fit at the waist); or quarter waist plus
4·5 cm (for an easy fit).
j is midway between h and C (centre of the
dart).
k is 10 cm below j.
l and m are 1 cm each side of j.
Join l–k–m for a second back dart.
The rest of the waistline is level with the top
edge of the paper.

To shape the side seam

d–n is quarter hip plus 0·5 cm (if you like a
close fit over the hips); or quarter hip plus
1 cm (for an easy fit).
p is 1 cm to the left of K.
q is 1 cm to the left of M.
Rule a straight line between h and n.
Rule a straight line between n and p.
Join h–n with a line curving up to 0·5 cm
outside the straight line.
Join n–p with a line curving up to 1 cm *inside*
the straight line.
Join p–q with a straight line.

To shape the inside-leg seam

r is 1 cm to the right of X.
s is 1 cm to the right of Y.
Rule a straight line between g and r.
Join g–r with a line curving up to 1·5 cm
inside the straight line.
Join r–s.

For the hemline

Join q–s with a shallow curve, dropping
0·5 cm at the centre, to the bottom edge of the
paper.

The heavy lines in *Figure 7* show the outline
of the back block pattern; mark this outline in
red to distinguish it easily from the front
block pattern.

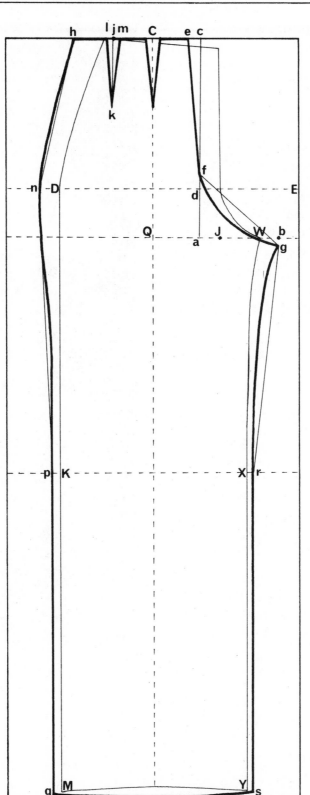

Figure 7

BACK

TRANSFERRING THE BLOCKS
TO CARD

Now that the block patterns have been drafted, you should transfer their outlines on to sheets of thin card.

Place the draft of the front block over a sheet of card and run the tracing wheel accurately round its outline. This will prick a line of perforations through to the card. Mark in the dart and the lines showing the hip and knee levels. Mark the line of the front leg crease; this will also be the straight-grain line when you cut the fabric. Cut out the card block.

Cut notches at each end of the hip line and of the knee line, to act as balance marks on the final pattern.

Repeat this for the back block, following the line marked in red. Then turn over the card and mark the lines on the reverse, so that the two blocks will both relate to the right-hand side of the body (*Figure 8*).

The blocks are now ready to be used for developing whatever style of trouser you may want. They themselves are not working patterns but templates: they are never cut or altered in any way. The final pattern, with all the design details as well as the seam and hem allowances, will be traced from them.

The blocks should last indefinitely. Drafting them is a once-for-all operation. To store them, punch a hole near the top of each block, thread a piece of tape through the holes and hang them from a coathanger. As your collection of block patterns for different types of garment grows, the coathangers can be hung flat at the back of a wardrobe where they will take up no space.

Flared trousers developed from the pattern blocks

Figure 8

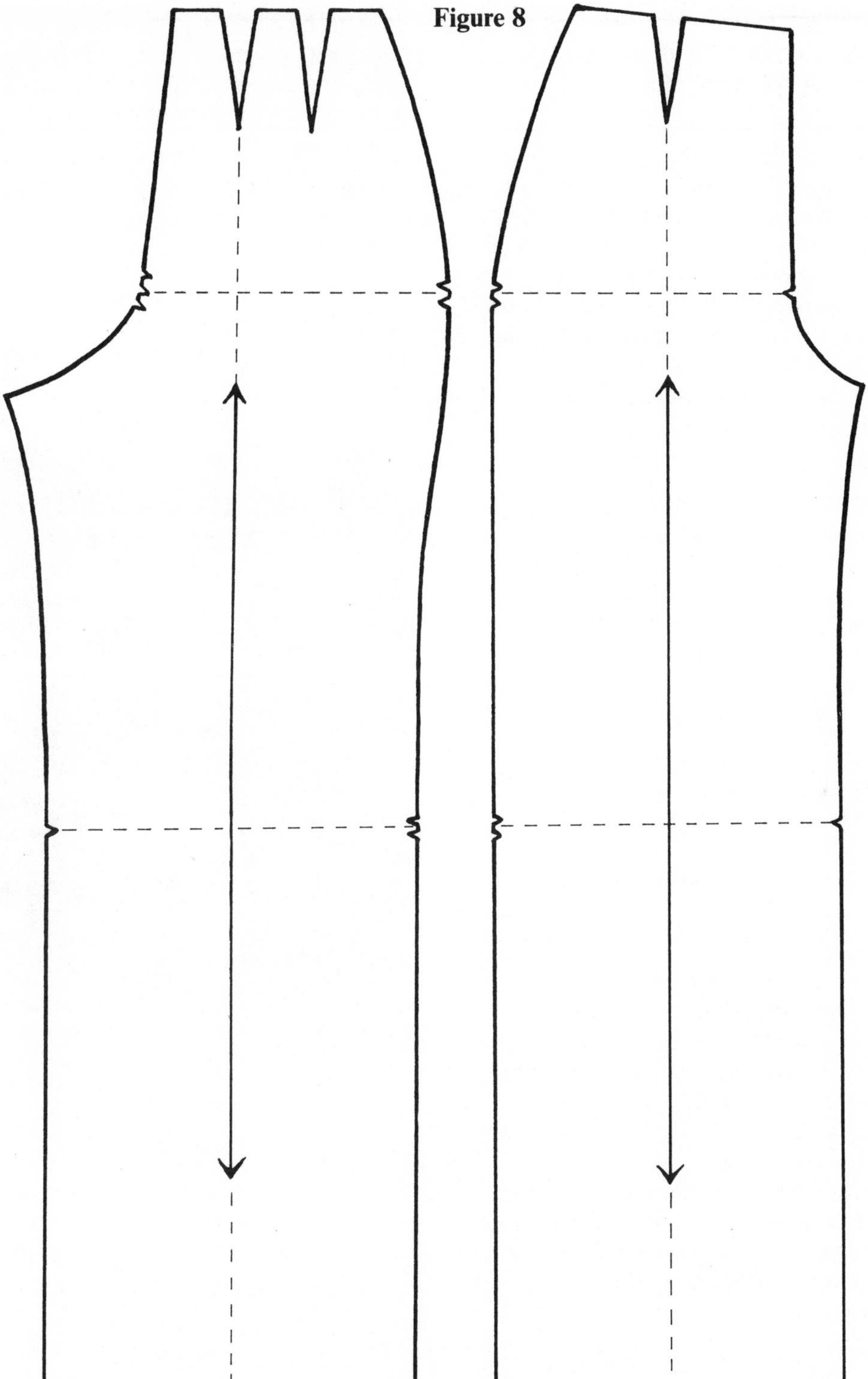

13

DESIGNING THE PATTERN

The geometry safely out of the way, the next step is to consider the style of trouser you are ready to develop from the blocks.

Will they be straight-legged, flared or tapered trousers – or will they be shorts? With or without turn-ups? Do you want a yoke at the back or front, or both, and will the trousers fit the waist or be cut as hipsters? Do you envisage a peg-top shape, with pleated fullness – or evening trousers in a silky fabric gathered into the waist and possibly, harem-fashion, into ankle bands? If you like any detail in trousers you already have, such as the style or size of a pocket, you could measure and copy it.

This section gives instructions for cutting a wide variety of styles. It is suggested that rather than read the section right through you just browse through the diagrams, for ideas. At *Figure 9* there is a group of body outlines; on thin paper placed over these, you could trace and then sketch in the effect of different styles until you have evolved a complete design.

Take plenty of time deciding: it is quite easy at this stage to work out a pattern for any design – much more difficult, and possibly wasteful in material, to change your ideas later on.

THE DRAFT PATTERN
You do not use the blocks directly as patterns. Their outlines are transferred on to new sheets of paper. On these you add whatever styling you want. You may have to cut the draft pattern into several pieces, in order to add a yoke or the fullness of a pleat. If so, the final outline is drawn round the pattern pieces on yet another sheet of paper. Lastly, seam and hem allowances are added, and the final pattern is cut out. An example of the whole process is shown in the photograph which appears on page 16.

1 Begin by cutting a strip of paper long enough to give a good margin at the top and bottom of the block. It will, in any case, be wide enough to accommodate the widest of trouser legs.

2 Draw round the outline of each block and mark in the hipline, kneeline and centre crease.

3 Beginning with the leg shape, work through the design features you want to include, in the order they are given below. Just pick out the instructions for the particular details you need and disregard the rest.

Tapered trousers developed from the pattern blocks

14

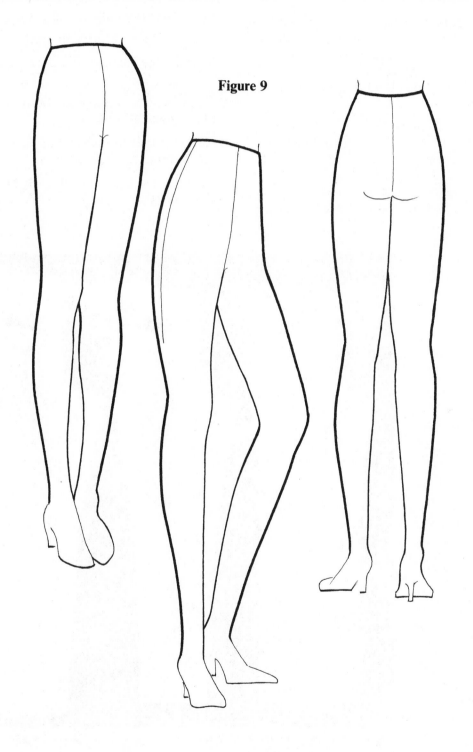

Figure 9

THE LEG SHAPE

Parallel trousers

From a close fit at hip level, the trousers fall straight, giving a fairly wide leg style. This is the basic shape of the blocks, so you will not need to make any alterations to the outline you have traced.

Trousers flared from the knee

The pattern will need to be widened between the hemline and the knee (*Figure 10*). No alteration is made above the knee. The trousers shown on page 12, for instance, have a standard knee width but measure 68 cm round the hem; 33 cm across front and 35 cm across the back leg. This is about as much flare as will hang well.

1 Decide the hem width you want.

2 Measure the hemlines traced from the blocks.

3 The difference is the extra width to be added. Divide this by four.

4 Add a quarter to each end of the back and to each end of the front hemline.

5 Rule the new leg seams, shaping the line into a smooth curve at knee level.

6 Redraw the hemline curve.

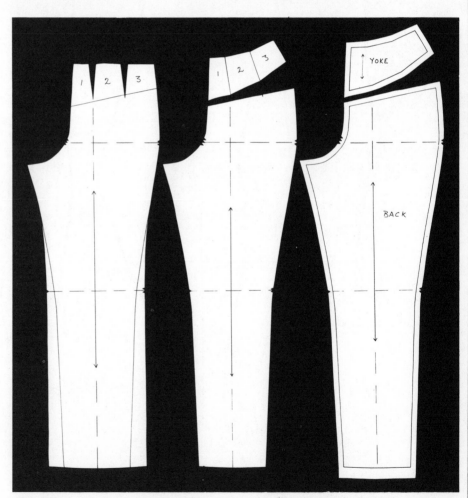

The stages of drafting the pattern for the tapered trousers shown on page 14

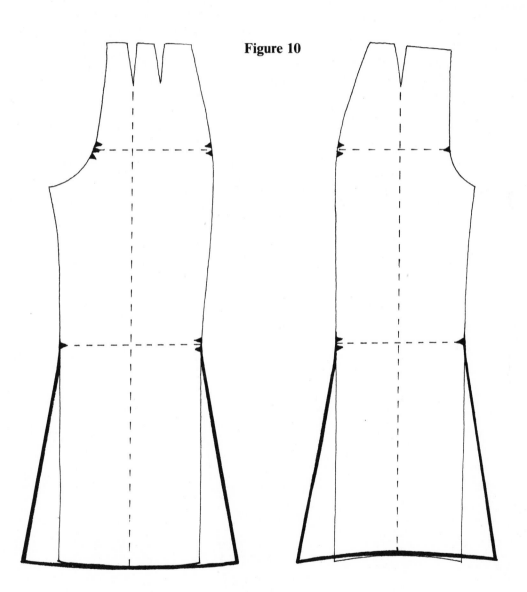

Figure 10

Fully-flared trousers

A very full trouser leg can be flared out from the crotch level (*Figure 11*). Again, decide the width needed at the hemline. This could, if you wish, be even as much as a metre; in a soft fabric, the trousers would then fall in folds like a flared skirt.

1 As above, work out the extra width needed at the hemline, and add a quarter to each end of the back and front hemlines.

2 Rule new side seamlines from hip level downwards.

3 Rule new inside leg seamlines from 4 cm below the crotch. Do not add any width to the crotch itself.

4 The new seamlines must be the same length as the old ones; so a wide flare will raise the bottom corners of the pattern and alter the hemline curve.

5 Redraw the hemline curve accordingly.

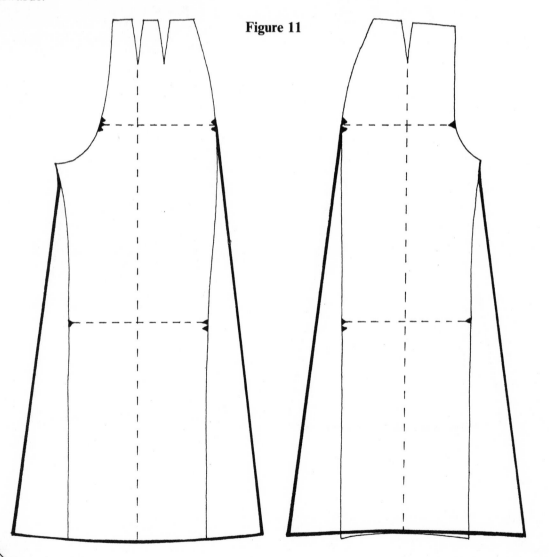

Figure 11

DESIGNING THE PATTERN

Tapered trousers

The pattern will need to be narrowed from the knee downwards (*Figure 12*). The trousers illustrated on page 14 measure only 38 cm round the bottoms: 18 cm across the front and 20 cm across the back. If made much narrower than this, they would be impractical because, without an ankle opening, they would not pull on easily over the foot.

1 Decide the hem measurement wanted.

2 Measure the hemlines traced from the blocks.

3 The difference is the width to be taken out. Divide this by four.

4 Subtract one quarter from each end of the back and of the front hemlines.

5 Redraw the leg seams from hem to knee, being careful to leave a smooth line at knee level.

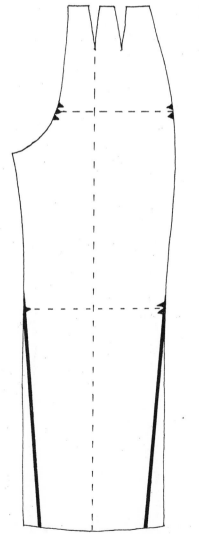

Figure 12

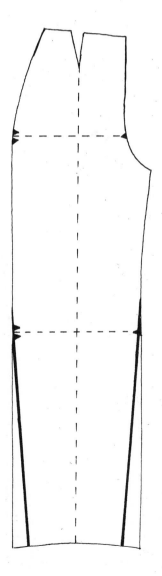

Thigh-fitting trousers

The blocks are fairly generously cut round the thigh (*Figure 13*). If you want trousers that fit closely above the knee, it is best to cut your pattern to the block shape and then, when you have cut out the fabric, to tack up and try on one leg. The side seam and inside leg seam should be taken in equally, always leaving a smooth line without any sudden bumps. Do not make any alteration to the crotch. Quite small reductions – 0·5 cm on each edge, for instance – will make a deal of difference to the fit.

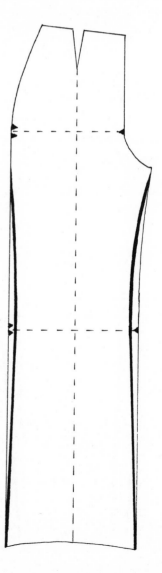

Figure 13

DESIGNING THE PATTERN

Tight-legged trousers in jersey fabric
Where the fabric is a stretchable jersey, you could make trousers that are virtually skin-tight; this is not possible with a woven fabric (*Figure 14*).

1 Decide, by measuring the leg, the minimum width required round the thigh (about 8 cm down from the crotch), round the knee and round the ankle. Make sure that your foot will pass through the ankle measurement.

2 Measure the pattern widths at these levels, and subtract a quarter of the difference from each edge.

3 Draw in the new side seamlines as shown, taking them up to within 10 cm of the waistline.

4 The crotch position should be moved 1 cm upwards and 1 cm inwards, and the inside leg seams taken up to join it.

5 A tight trouser leg should clear the instep; the leg will therefore have to be shortened by up to 5 cm. However, this is an alteration that can be done more accurately on the figure, after the trousers have been made up.

Figure 14

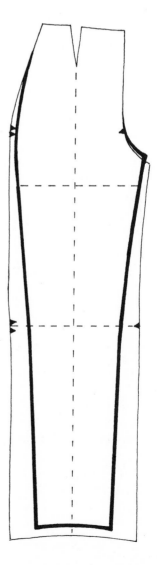

DESIGNING THE PATTERN

Shorts

The standard block is suitable for shorts of any length, from the extremely brief down to knee-length Bermudas (*Figure 15*).

1 Trace round the blocks as far down as necessary for the length you plan. Mark in the hip lines and, if applicable, the knee lines.

2 At the chosen hem level, rule a line across both patterns, parallel to these lines.

3 Curve the hemline down 1 cm across the back.

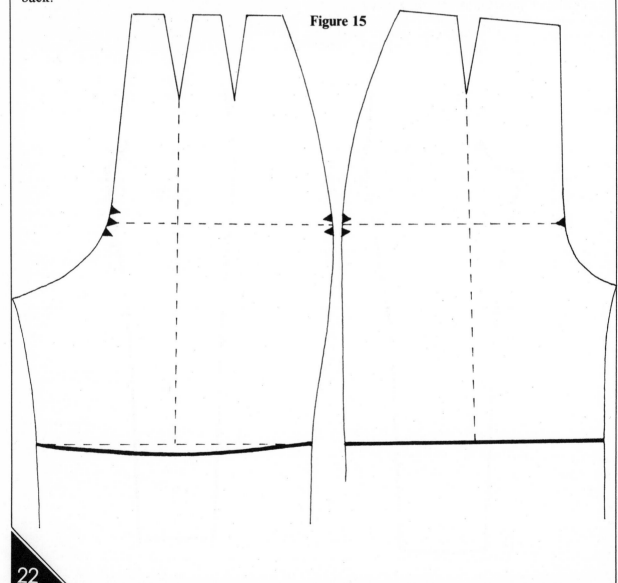

Figure 15

DESIGNING THE PATTERN

Very brief shorts will hang better with a little more fullness at the back. For this alteration:

1 Cut out the back pattern.

2 Cut up the crease line to the point of the dart, and separate the pattern into two pieces (*Figure 16*).

Figure 16

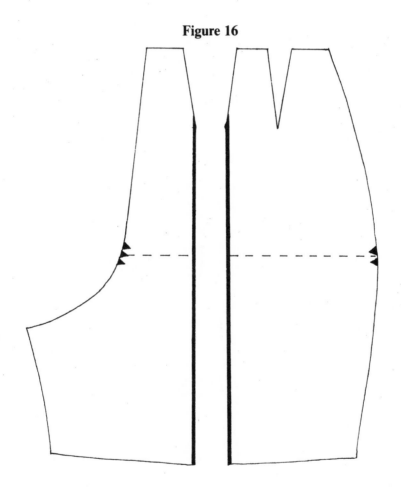

3 Swing the pieces round to close the dart; this will open up 5–8 cm extra width at the hemline, depending on the length of the shorts (*Figure 17*).

4 Pin the two pattern pieces on to fresh paper and trace round. The new pattern will now have only one back dart. Extend the closed dart line downwards to give the new crease line for the back of the shorts.

5 Connect the two parts of the hemline with a shallow curve.

6 No alteration is needed to the front pattern.

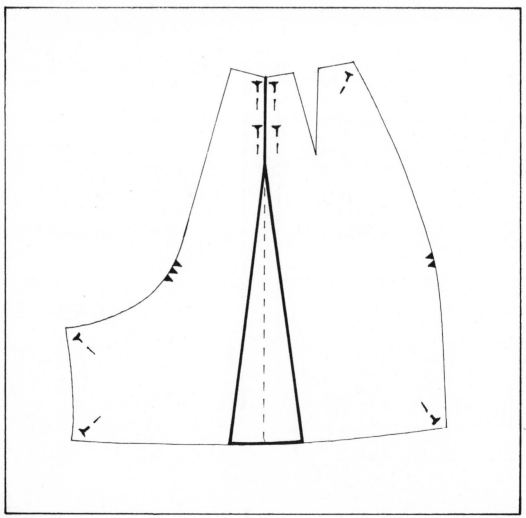

Figure 17

TURN-UPS

The depth of a turn-up should be 4 cm so, being in double thickness, it will add 8 cm to the trouser length. Forget for the moment the hem allowance.

For parallel trousers

Lengthen the leg seamlines of the pattern by 8 cm. Omit the curve at the hemline.

For slightly shaped trousers

Whether these are flared or tapered, the hemline curve is again omitted, but the ends of the turn-up must be shaped.

1 Rule two lines parallel to the pattern hemline, one 4 cm and the other 8 cm below it (*Figure 18*).

2 Cut the pattern along the lower line.

3 Crease the pattern and fold along the upper line and again along the hemline (*Figure 19*).

4 Cut through the folds along the dotted lines, across the turn-up.

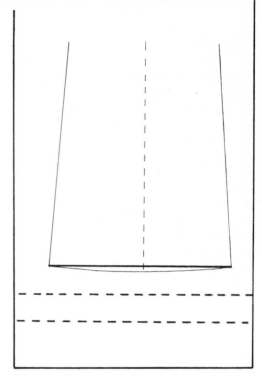

Figure 18

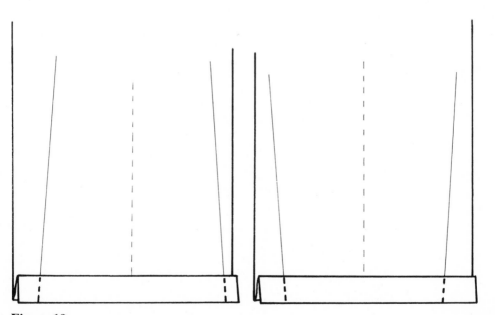

Figure 19

5 The unfolded pattern will be as shown in *Figure 20*.

For widely flared trousers
Any turn-up would tend to flap away from the leg in an ugly line. In any case, it would have to be shaped and cut separately, with a separate facing. Not recommended.

THE WAIST LEVEL

The blocks are designed for trousers that fit closely at the natural waistline. If, however, you want hipsters, the alteration is simple. From the traced outlines, simply rule and cut off 6 cm at top of back and front (*Figure 21*). The darts at both back and front will be shortened, but the fit will remain unaltered.

Hipsters need a narrow waistband – no more than 2·5 cm wide – to sit well on the hip. Instructions for cutting waistbands are on page 38.

YOKES

A back yoke is an essential part of the design of jeans; but front or back yokes can be used on any trousers. They are a good waist finish for fully gathered trousers. If you wish to dispense with a waistband, the yoke could be mounted directly on to petersham ribbon (US grosgrain), turned to the inside of the waistline.

Remember that there will be a seam down the centre-front and centre-back. Although it is possible to cut a yoke in one piece (with the opening at the side seam), this would allow no fitting adjustments. It is better to plan yokes with centre seams.

The most pleasing shape and depth of a yoke is not easy to judge on paper; it may help you to mark the proposed outline with tailor's chalk on a pair of existing trousers, to see how it looks on the figure.

The photograph on page 8 shows a typical back yoke for jeans, below a waistband. This yoke measured 6 cm deep at the side seam, dropping to 10 cm deep at centre-back. A front yoke could be cut deeper – say up to 14 cm at the centre.

1 Draw the line of the yoke on the trouser patterns. (The depth of the back and front yokes should match at the side seam.)

2 Cut the pattern along this line (*Figure 22*). (If the last centimetre at the point of a dart is left on the top of the trouser section, it can be disregarded.)

3 Close the dart shapings in the yoke (*Figure 23*).

4 On fresh paper, draw round the altered yoke pattern. Mark in a straight-grain arrow parallel to the centre-back or centre-front (*Figure 24*).

Figure 20

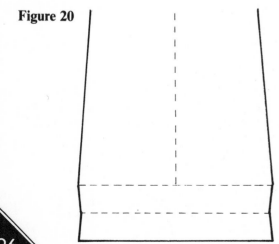
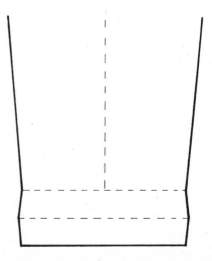

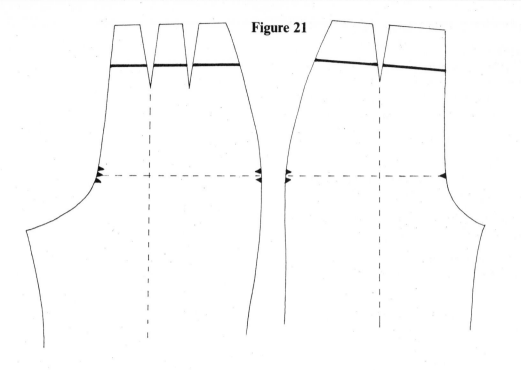

Figure 21

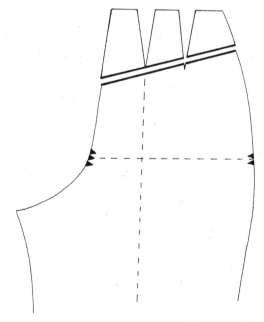

Figure 22

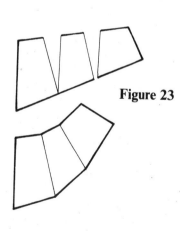

Figure 23

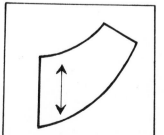

Figure 24

TROUSERS WITH BODY FULLNESS

Waistline pleats

On the front pattern only, a peg-top effect can be achieved with unstitched pleats springing from the waistline. This style would look well with a waistband 4–5 cm wide (*Figure 25*).

1 Cut out the traced pattern of the trouser front.

2 Mark A midway between the dart and the side edge of the waistline (*Figure 26*).

3 On the side edge mark B, 25 cm down from the waist; mark C, 5 cm lower.

4 Cut the pattern from A to 0·2 cm short of B. Cut from the point of dart to 0·2 cm short of C.

5 Open up the dart until it is 5 cm wide at the waistline.

Figure 25

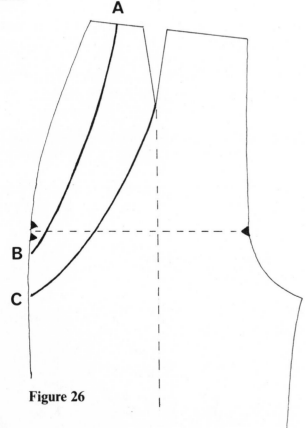

Figure 26

6 Open up the line A–B until the gap at A is 5 cm wide (*Figure 27*).

7 On fresh paper, draw round the altered pattern, leaving a margin along the top edge.

8 Now fold in a pair of 5 cm pleats, at the dart and at A. If you fold as shown in *Figure 25*, with the pleats sloping nicely towards the side, you will find that the waistline has become distorted. Pin the pleats in place and cut a new, smooth line for the waist (*Figure 28*).

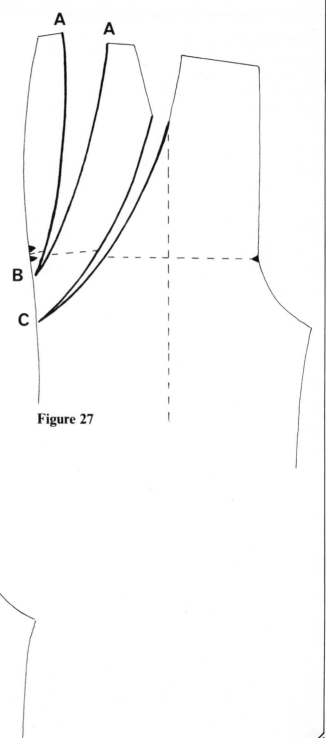

Figure 27

Figure 28

9 The unfolded pattern will be shaped as in
Figure 29.

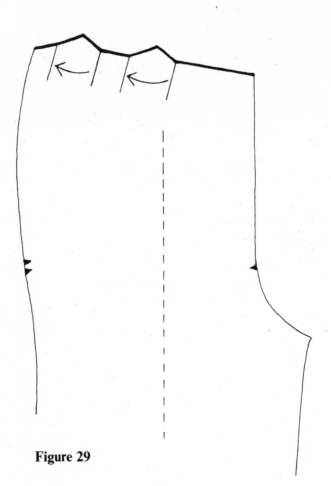

Figure 29

Waistline gathers

Evening trousers in a fine, silky fabric can be
cut with extra fullness down their whole
length. The fullness is gathered into a
waistband or a yoke. The pattern for this type
of trouser is simple to draft, the only difficulty
being to judge just how much fullness will
look best with the particular fabric you are
using. Some will need as little as 4–5 cm extra
width added to the back and front
measurements; others, such as fine polyester
jerseys, will hang beautifully with gatherings
of 10 cm or more.

The solution is to try draping the uncut fabric
on the figure. Take one end of your fabric and
run gathering threads across from selvage to
selvage. Pull up the threads, then hold the
gathers to your waist to see the effect of
different degrees of fullness.

For a style gathered from a waistband:

1 Cut the pattern down the crease line (*Figure 30*).

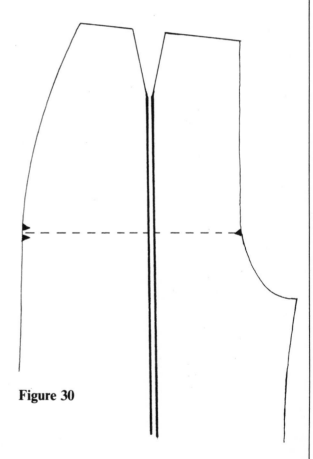

Figure 30

DESIGNING THE PATTERN

2 Spread the pattern pieces apart, keeping the hiplines level and the cut edges parallel down the whole length of the trouser leg. Add as much width as you wish, bearing in mind that there should be no gathers within 4 cm of the centre or side seam edges.

3 On fresh paper, redraw the new outline, deleting the dart placings (*Figure 31*).

4 Repeat for the other trouser section.

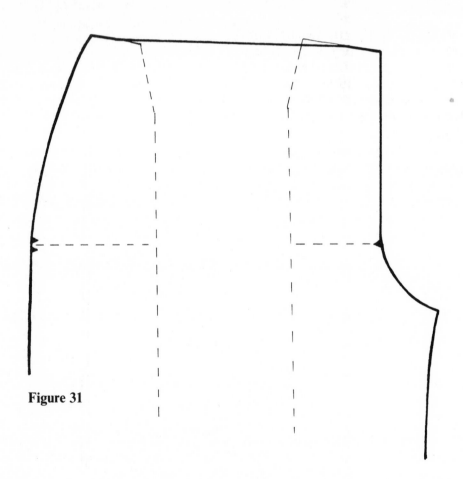

Figure 31

For gathers falling from a yoke – which usually look better than those falling directly from a waistband – first cut the yoke away from the main pattern piece. Then cut apart and spread the trouser sections, redrawing the upper edge as in *Figure 32*. Mark notches as shown – the gathers will be between them.

Trousers gathered into ankle bands
Gathered trousers lend themselves well to this finish.

The amount of fullness in the leg will be limited to what will gather, without undue bulk, into the ankle bands. This depends on the fabric; you will be able to manage more width in a very thin synthetic jersey than in any woven fabric. Taper the trouser legs from the knee if necessary, as shown in *Figure 12*.

Cut the band pattern to the length that easily fits your ankle, plus 3–4 cm for an underlap. The depth could be between 4 and 8 cm.

The trousers themselves may need to be shortened; or else the extra length could be bloused over the band. Make no alteration to the length of the pattern – make up the trousers first and then, on the figure, you will be able to judge the best length.

An alternative finish would be with a casing for elastic. This tends to look bulky, but saves time if you want to wear the trousers tonight.

Elasticated trousers
Easy-fitting trousers with an elasticated waistband and no opening are possible only in stretchable fabrics. Cut the back and front from the unaltered block patterns, marking the same darts. When the trousers are tacked up, you will be able to test whether they can be pulled easily over the hips; if not, the side-back dart can be narrowed or dispensed with.

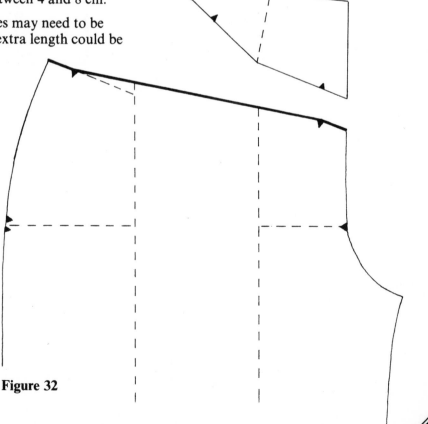

Figure 32

33

POCKETS

Patch pockets

On jeans, a pair of these pockets below the back yoke seam is pretty well obligatory. They would be decorated according to current fancy with double lines of top-stitching, with metal brads or with any applied motif. But patch pockets can equally well be designed for any trousers. They need not be rectangular; their lower edge could be cut to a point, or their corners be rounded.

The proportion of the pocket to the figure, and the level at which it is to be applied, are both important to the finished look of the trousers. Try chalking the pocket outlines on a pair of existing trousers to test the effect.

Cut the draft pocket pattern to its finished size. Place it on the trouser pattern and draw round it to mark its final position. *Figure 33* shows the position of a back pocket on a pair of jeans – one side of it should be matched to the crease line, and the pocket itself cut with a sloping edge to fit directly below the yoke seam.

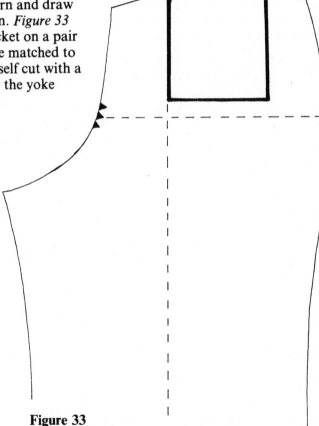

Figure 33

DESIGNING THE PATTERN

Patch pockets from side seams

This type of pocket – very simple to apply – has two edges top-stitched to the front trouser section. The top edge is taken into the waist finish and the remaining side taken into the side seam (*Figure 34*). Again, the size, shape and proportion of such pockets are vital to the finished appearance of the trousers.

Mark the proposed outline on the trouser front section. The pocket could conveniently extend to the crease line. Its opening edge should be no more than 15 cm, and its lower edge where it looks right – probably below the hipline. Trace the pocket shape from the trouser section and cut out the pocket pattern. Mark in the hipline notch on the pocket pattern. The lining is cut to the same pattern.

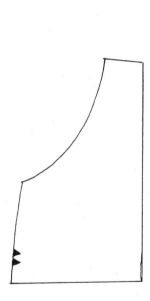

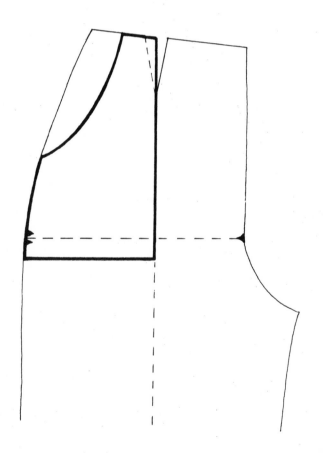

Figure 34

Trouser side pockets

A standard trouser pocket is not unduly difficult to set and can be an attractive point of the design. It should have a fairly short opening edge, to prevent gaping. The width of your hand plus 3 cm is long enough – say 11–12 cm. The top end of the opening should be set 2–3 cm forward from the side seam.

1 On the trouser front pattern, draw the line of the pocket opening, A–B (*Figure 35*).

2 Draw the shape of the pocket bag – about 12 cm wide by 24 cm deep.

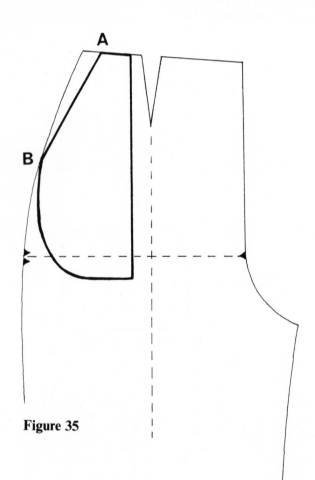

Figure 35

3 Trace one pocket piece with an edge slanting from A to B; this will be cut from lining fabric. Trace one pocket piece shaped out to the side seamline; this will be cut from the trouser fabric (*Figure 36*).

4 Trim the trouser pattern along the pocket opening line A–B (*Figure 37*). Discard the little wedge.

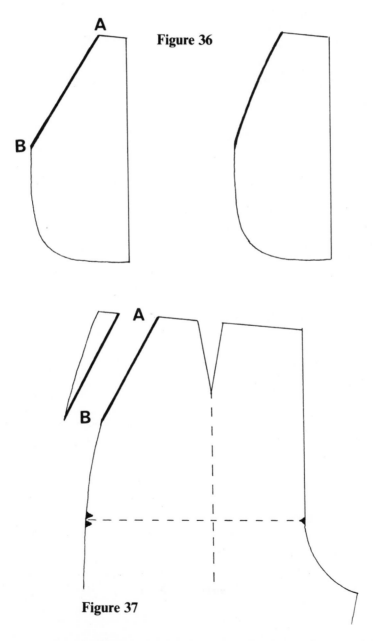

Figure 36

Figure 37

THE ZIP

A zip can be set at the front, back or side. In closely-fitted trousers, a side zip is not really satisfactory because of the curve of the hip. A back zip is less used in trousers than in skirts, but is a good choice if a clean line is wanted across the front.

Most trousers have the zip set at the centre-front. No alteration is needed to the pattern for an ordinary zip setting, but a fly-front design needs an extension from the waistline downwards, 4 cm wide by 20 cm long. Draw this on the front trouser pattern (*Figure 38*).

THE WAIST FINISH

A very firm waistline, provided by a waistband or petersham, is needed on fitted trousers. A waistline facing is not really strong enough for the job.

Petersham ribbon

Turned to the inside, petersham gives an invisible waist mounting; this is the best finish where you wish to avoid cluttering the design. No alteration is needed to the pattern for a petersham waist finish.

Waistbands

On most trousers a waistband is used. The simplest kind, a narrow band up to 5 cm wide, can be cut straight (as in the photographs on pages 12 and 14). It should be the length of the trouser waist, plus 3 cm for an underlap if needed. Cut it double the finished width. Mark notches on it to show the positions of the trouser seams (*Figure 39*).

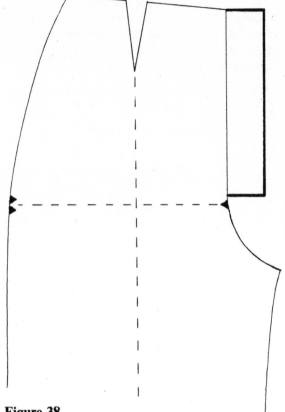

Figure 38

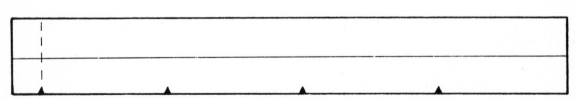

Figure 39

DESIGNING THE PATTERN

Waistbands wider than 5 cm should be shaped to the waist. If the upper edge of a deep band is to be set on the natural waistline, its lower edge will need to be longer to fit the top of the hip.

1 Decide the width of the waistband.

2 Trim that amount from the waistline of the two trouser sections (*Figure 40*).

3 Fold in and pin the darts on these pieces, and match them together at the side seam.

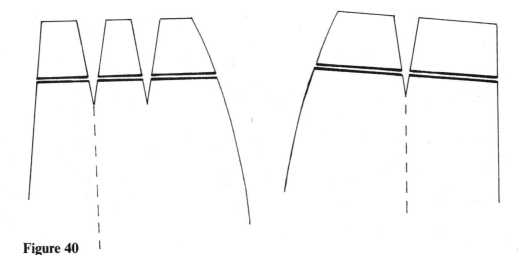

Figure 40

DESIGNING THE PATTERN

4 Fold your pattern drafting paper in half (*Figure 41*). Working from the fold, towards the right, trace the waistband pieces from centre-back to centre-front in one continuous curve.

5 Cut along the top and bottom of the waistband pattern and unfold the paper.

6 Cut the right-hand end level with the traced pattern, but allow an underlap of 3 cm at the left-hand end.

7 Mark with notches the positions where the seams will meet the waistband (*Figure 42*).

8 A second waistband, from the same pattern, will be needed as a facing.

As this waistband incorporates much of the dart shaping, the darts remaining on the trouser sections are automatically shortened.

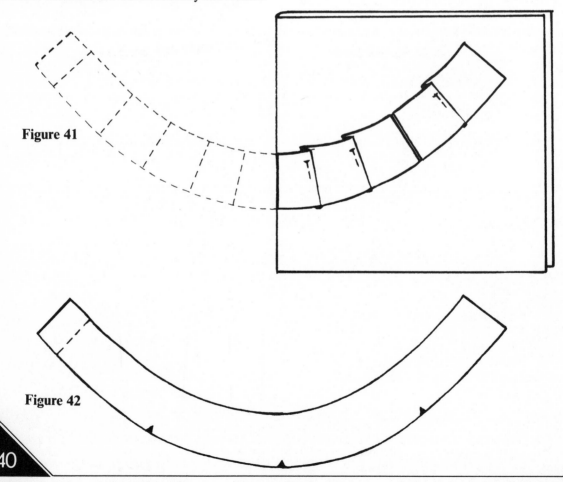

Figure 41

Figure 42

Elasticated waistbands

These are used for jersey trousers with no front opening. Cut the band 4 cm longer than the trouser waistline (as you may need to let out the darts) and make sure it will pull on easily over your hips.

Belt carriers

Cut these from scraps. A carrier should be as long as the width of the waistband (plus turnings) and four times its own finished width. It is convenient to make them as one continuous strip, folded and machined, and afterwards cut up into lengths.

For jeans, five carriers are usual – at the centre-back and above the four crease lines (*Figure 43*).

SEAM AND HEM ALLOWANCES

The pattern has been drafted 'net', without any turnings. The edges of the pattern pieces all coincide with seamlines or with the length of a finished edge. Now, with all the pieces drafted, is the time to add seam and hem allowances, as in the photograph on page 16.

1 Add 1·5 cm to:
the waistline edges;
the side seams and inside-leg seams;
the centre-back and centre-front seams (including any zip extension).

2 Add 1·5 cm to all the edges of the waistband, the yokes and the pocket pieces. Add 2·5 cm to the opening edge of a patch pocket to act as a facing.

3 The depth of the hem allowance depends on the fabric, and the cut of the trousers:
for parallel or gathered trousers, add 4 cm;
for trousers with turn-ups, add 3 cm;
for tapered or slightly flared trousers, add 3 cm;
for shorts, add 3 cm;
for widely-flared trousers, add 2 cm;
for trousers with ankle bands, add 1·5 cm.

Draw or rule at these distances outside all the pattern outlines and cut out. Mark notches along the new edges. Check that the names of the pieces, and straight-grain lines, are marked on all of them.

These are the final patterns, ready for laying out on the fabric.

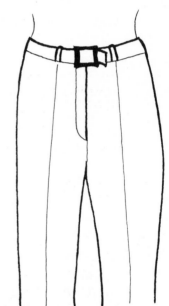

Figure 43

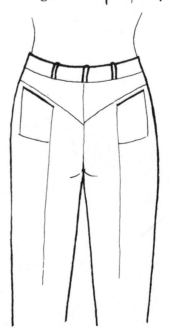

DESIGNING THE PATTERN

FABRIC REQUIREMENTS

As you are not working with a commercial pattern you will not have the guidance, given on the pattern envelope, as to the length of fabric needed.

So first choose your fabric, note its width and also any check or surface texture that may have to be matched. Next, make a pattern layout to see show much you will need to buy. Only then, buy the fabric.

The pattern layout

Unless you have a really large table, plan the layout of the pattern pieces on the floor.

1 Take the width of the fabric when folded in half, with the selvages matched. Use the edge of a carpet to represent the fold of the fabric, and a long ruler or straight edge, placed parallel to it and the appropriate distance away, to represent the selvage edges.

2 Place your pattern pieces, as economically as possible, with the straight-grain arrows parallel to the edges (*Figure 44*).

3 Check the number of pattern pieces you will need. As your fabric will be folded, you will automatically cut two of each piece. But you will need four pieces for lined patch pockets, and for ankle bands; so patterns for these will have to be cut twice over.

FOLD

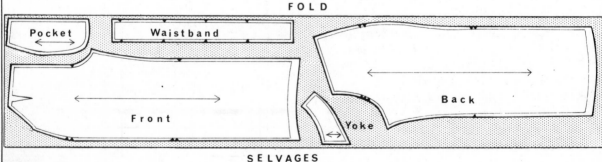

SELVAGES

Figure 44

4 If you have chosen a napped fabric – such as corduroy – with a one-way surface texture, or a material with a one-way design, then all the pattern pieces must be laid with their tops towards the same end of the layout. An uneven check, such as the one shown in *Figure 45*, must be treated in the same way.

5 If the fabric is checked, add one complete repeat of the pattern to the measured length of your layout, to allow precise matching.

The fabric and notions

Only now are you ready to calculate the length needed, and buy the fabric. At the same time, buy what Americans call the 'notions' – the necessary bits and pieces to make up the garment:

18 or 20 cm metal-toothed zip;
matching thread and if necessary buttonhole twist for top-stitching;
waistline hook and bar;
seam binding or bias binding, for hems;
a strip of interfacing for the waistband (heavy iron-on Vilene is suitable), or 2·5 cm-wide petersham;
30 cm of lining fabric for pocket bags;
tape for pocket-edge reinforcement.

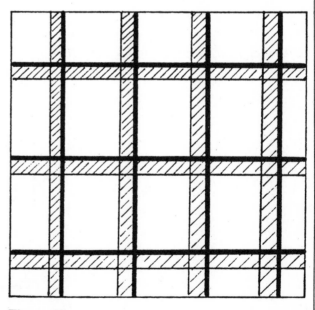

Figure 45

From here on, all is plain sailing.

The instructions that follow give the sequence in which you should work, whatever type of trouser you are making. As you go along, pick out the instructions for your particular design and disregard the rest.

CUTTING OUT
Fold the fabric lengthwise, with the right side inside. It is important that the selvages (or stripes) be perfectly matched, so that the fold is exactly on the straight-grain of the fabric.

Place the pattern pieces in the positions you have planned, with their straight-grain arrows parallel to the selvages. (With a check, plan the trouser creases to run down the most conspicuous stripe.) Smooth the pieces down their centres, hold them with one pin at each end, check the straight-grain arrow again and then smooth out and pin down the corners. Finally, pin all round the edges at intervals of 10–15 cm.

Cut out. When you come to a notch, cut outwards, not into the seam allowance; you might need that width to let out a seam (*Figure 46*).

Leave the patterns pinned to the trouser pieces.

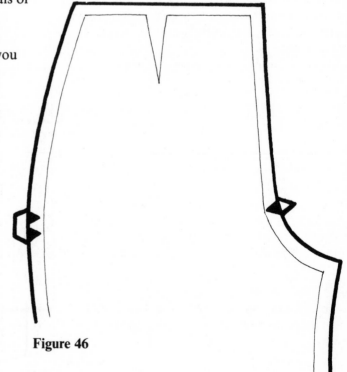

Figure 46

MARKING

The patterns already have their seam allowances marked round the fitting lines. It is extremely important that your seams are stitched precisely along these lines, or the fit will be affected. So mark the vital points, through the pattern on to the fabric, as a guide for your machining. There are several ways to do this.

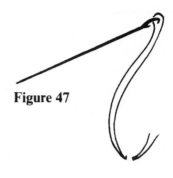

Figure 47

Dressmaker's carbon paper

Insert the carbon paper (face downwards) between the pattern and the upper layer of fabric; place another carbon (face upwards) under the lower layer. On a firm surface, mark through the pattern with the tracing wheel, making a cross at the point to be marked. The marks will be transferred to the wrong side of the fabric.

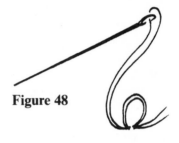

Figure 48

Tailor's tacks

This method is nearly as quick, and rather more reliable, since carbon markings may not show up well on rough-surfaced fabrics.

Figure 49

1 Using a double thread, take a tiny stitch through the pattern and both thicknesses of fabric, at the point to be marked (*Figure 47*).

2 Take another stitch through the same point, and leave a loop big enough to put your finger through (*Figure 48*).

3 Cut the thread, leaving 1 cm ends (*Figure 49*).

4 When you have marked all the points on the pattern piece, gently tear off the pattern. If your stitches were small, so will the holes be. Then ease apart the two layers of fabric, and cut the loops of thread between them (*Figure 50*).

5 You will be left with tufts of thread in each piece of fabric, which can be matched with their opposite numbers when you pin the seams.

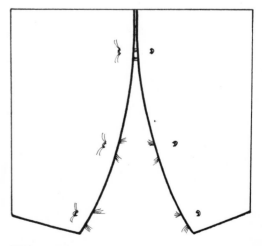

Figure 50

MAKING UP THE TROUSERS

Points to be marked

1 The points where seamlines cross – the corners at the waistline and at the crotch.

2 Dart markings, at the seamline and at the point. Pleat markings, at the seamline and again 5 cm down the pleat.

3 The level of the stop-end of the zip. To mark this on the centre-front seam, measure the opening length of the zip, down from the waist fitting line.

4 The trouser crease lines, at knee level and at the bottom.

5 The corners of patch pocket placings.

FITTING

Even though the pattern has been cut to your exact measurements, the fitting of the trousers on the figure itself is essential for a perfect result. For this, you must have the help of a friend to make any alterations – while you stand up straight.

1 Tack the darts (*Figure 51*). Tack across any pleats, to hold them in place (*Figure 52*).

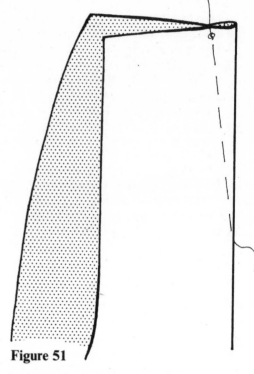

Figure 51

Figure 52

2 Press under the lower edge of any yoke piece, and tack it (from the right side) over the corresponding trouser section, matching the yoke fold to the fitting line (*Figure 53*).

3 Press under the side and inside-leg seam allowances of the *front* trouser sections. Lap the folded edge of the front section over the edge of the back section, matching the fitting lines. Tack the seams and press them (*Figure 54*).

4 Turn up and pin the hemline of the trouser bottoms.

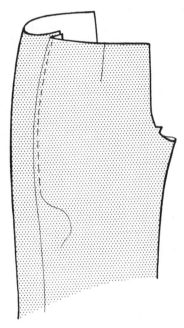

Figure 54

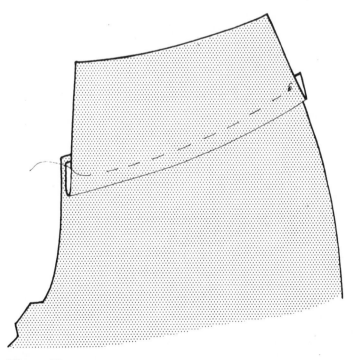

Figure 53

5 You now have two separate legs. Turn one of them wrong-side-out; push the other one (right-side-out) inside it. Tack the centre-back and centre-front seam as one continuous seam, as far as the zip marking (*Figure 55*). (This seamline should not need to be altered in fitting, so it is not tacked from the right side like the other seams.)

6 Turn the trousers right-side-out. Pin the waistband – or a tape – round the waistline. Try on the trousers and pin together the opening.

Fitting the waist
Make sure that the waistband holds the trousers comfortably up to the crotch and that there is no sagging below the waistline; *Figure 56* shows a bad case. To correct this, take up any slack at centre-front or back into the waistband.

If the trousers pull at any point on the waist, as in *Figure 57*, raise the waistband at that point.

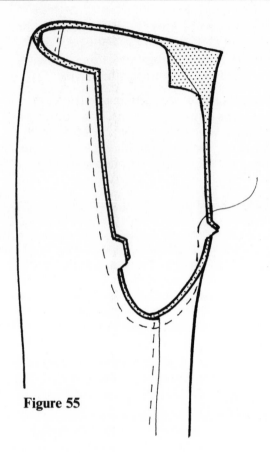

Figure 55

Figure 56

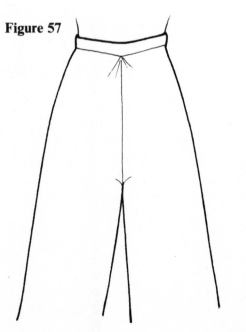

Figure 57

MAKING UP THE TROUSERS

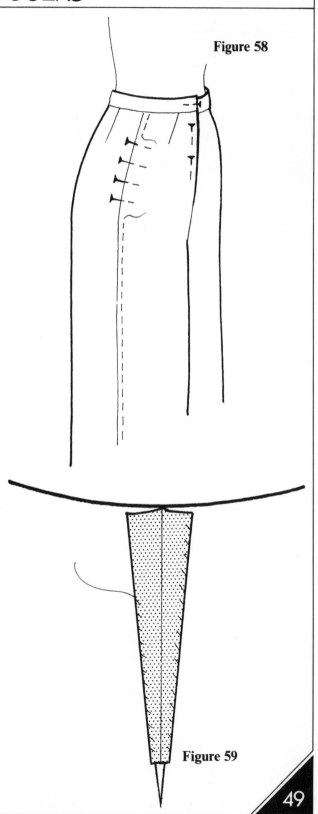

Figure 58

From the side, check that the trousers hang vertically, with the side seams down the centre of the leg. If they hang with the seam slanting towards the toes, lift the *back* waistline and re-pin it a little higher into the waistband. If the trousers hang towards the back, with the seam slanting to the heel, lift the *front* of the waistline slightly.

Check that the darts are the right length for your figure. If they pull at the points, shorten them. If they pout out at the ends, pin them slightly longer to take in a little more fabric.

Fitting the hips
Now you can judge the fitting over the hips. Women vary greatly in this curve, and it is essential to make any small alterations on the figure. Just snip the side seam tacking at the point to be altered, move the folded front edge to the right position over the unfolded back edge, and pin the altered seamline in place (*Figure 58*). (This right-side tacking considerably simplifies the operation.)

The leg shape
Is the width round the thigh and knee as you want it? This again is much easier to judge on the figure. If necessary, snip the tacking and alter *both* the side *and* the inside-leg seams equally. Do not make any alteration at crotch.

Now take off the trousers, re-tack, trim off any surplus at the seamline and try on again to check.

The length
Make sure that the length is as you want it and that the hemline is level or evenly sloped down towards the heel.

Lastly, take out the centre seam tacking to separate the two trouser legs.

THE DARTS
Stitch these first, and press them towards the centre. In thick fabric, they should be slashed, pressed open and the raw edges overcast (*Figure 59*). Now press in the back and front trouser creases, very thoroughly, from the dart downwards.

Figure 59

49

YOKES

Work any yoke seams next. Yokes look best
top-stitched; stitch from the right side, over
the existing tacking and close to the folded
edge of the yoke. Use buttonhole twist and
the longest machine stitch setting; then run a
second row of stitching, 1 cm above the first
(*Figure 60*).

For trousers gathered into yokes, run
gathering threads between the notches, pull
up to fit the notches on the yoke and work the
seam with right sides together (*Figure 61*).
Press the turnings upwards.

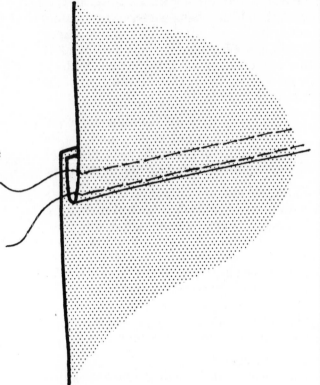

Figure 60

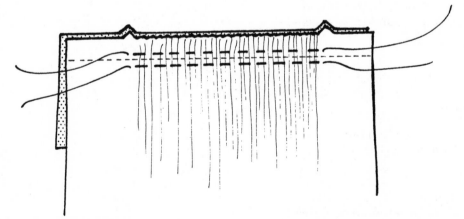

Figure 61

PATCH POCKETS

1 Finish the edge of the pocket facing with zigzag stitching.

2 Fold the facing over to the right side. Stitch as shown in *Figure 62,* across the facing and round the side and bottom edges.

3 Trim the seams and corners, turn the facing back to the wrong side, and press in the seam turnings (*Figure 63*).

4 Work any machine-stitched decoration on the hip patch pockets of jeans.

5 Tack the pockets to their marked positions on the trouser sections.

6 Top-stitch round the three pocket edges, beginning and ending with small triangles or squares of stitching, for a firm finish (*Figure 64*).

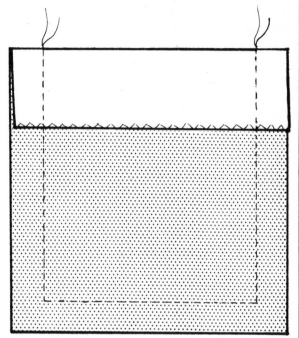

Figure 62

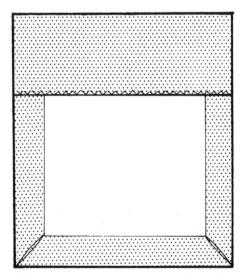

Figure 63

Figure 64

Patch pockets from side seams

1 Place pocket and lining pieces with right sides together. Stitch the longer side and the bottom as one seam. Stitch along the pocket mouth (*Figure 65*).

2 Trim the corner, clip any curves and turn the pocket right-side-out (*Figure 66*).
Top-stitch the pocket mouth if you wish.

3 Tack the pockets to their marked positions on the front trouser pieces, and top-stitch in place (*Figure 67*).

4 The unfinished pocket edges are later taken into the side and waist seams of the trousers.

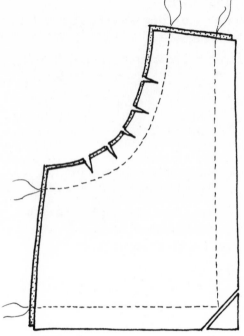

Figure 65

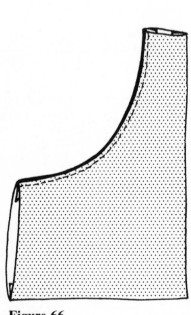

Figure 66

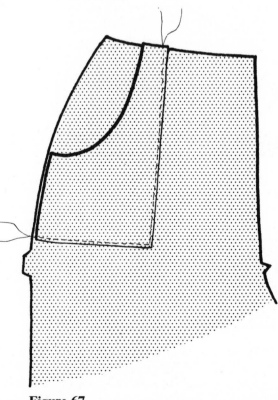

Figure 67

TROUSER SIDE POCKETS

1 With right sides together, match the slanting opening edge of the *lining* pocket piece to the slanting edge of the front trouser section. Strengthen this seam with tape and stitch it from the top corner of the pocket only as far down as the end of the opening – *not* into the seam allowance (*Figure 68*).

2 Press the seam out flat, and top-stitch the lining to the turnings, just inside the seamline (*Figure 69*).

3 With right sides together, match the *fabric* pocket piece to the back trouser section at waistline and side edges. Stitch this seam from the top only as far down as the end of the opening, not into the seam allowance (*Figure 70*).

4 Leave the finishing of the pockets until the side seams are stitched.

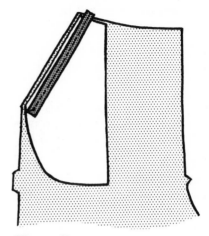

Figure 68

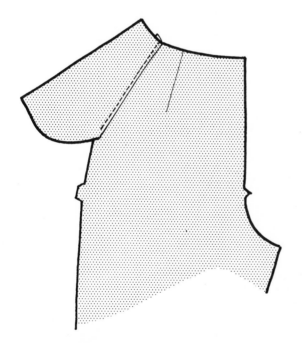

Figure 69

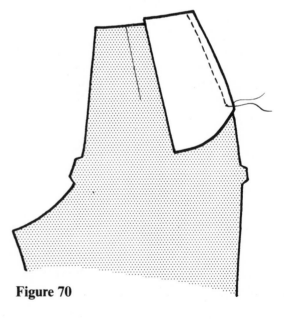

Figure 70

MAKING UP THE TROUSERS

SIDE SEAMS

If any part of a side seam was taken in during fitting, trim its turnings (before taking out the tacking) to an even 1·5 cm.

There are two ways of working these seams, depending on the style you have chosen.

Flat seams

Take out the tacking, place right sides together and stitch. Press open the turnings and finish with zigzag stitching (*Figure 71*).

Top-stitched seams

There is no need to take out the tacking; instead, remove the tacking from the inside-leg seam, to allow you to work the side seam on flat fabric.

Then top-stitch from the right side (with buttonhole twist and the longest stitch) close to the folded edge. Stitch again 1 cm forward from the first stitching (*Figure 72*). This type of seam is shown in the trousers on page 8; it is a good finish for jeans seams.

SEAMS WITH SIDE POCKETS

1 If you have a pocket in the side seam, stitch from the lower end of the pocket opening downwards (*Figure 73*). Do not catch in the pocket edges.

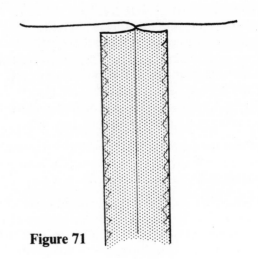

Figure 71

Figure 72

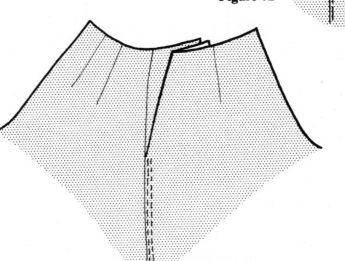

Figure 73

2 Now finish the pockets. Stitch together both halves of the pocket bag, from the side seam round the bottom and up the remaining side of the pocket (*Figure 74*). Clip the turning at the bottom of the pocket mouth, as shown, to allow the seams to lie flat.

3 On the right side, tack together the top edges of the pocket ready for setting into the waistband (*Figure 75*).

INSIDE-LEG SEAMS
These are not usually top-stitched, and are better worked as flat seams (*Figure 71*).

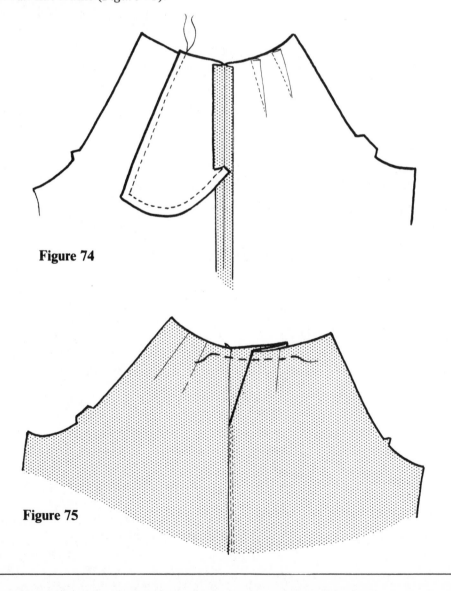

Figure 74

Figure 75

THE CROTCH SEAM

Now that both legs are complete, push one inside the other, as you did for the fitting, and stitch the crotch seam from the back waistline round to the zip marking in front of the crotch.

Press the turnings open down as far as the back notches, and finish their edges separately with zigzag stitching. Between the notches, lay the turnings together and stitch 0·5 cm from the seamline; trim to this second row of machining and finish with zigzag stitching over the edge (*Figure 76*).

THE ZIP

For a plain zip finish

(without fabric extensions)

1 Tack together the sides of the front opening along the seamline. Press the turnings open.

2 Pin the zip under the tacked seamline. If you pin from the right side, you can feel the position of the zipper chain through the fabric; pin it centrally behind the opening. Tack where you have pinned (*Figure 77*).

3 Working from the wrong side, with a zipper foot on the machine, stitch down the centre of one tape, across the bottom below the teeth, and up the other side (*Figure 78*). Remove the tackings.

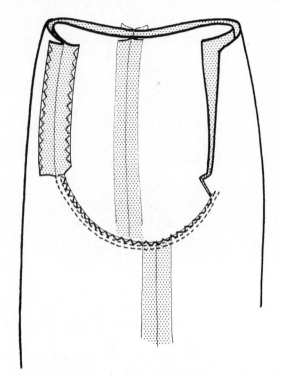

Figure 76

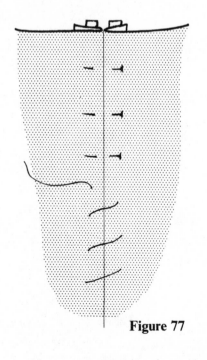

Figure 77

Figure 78

For a fly front
(Shown in the right and wrong side photographs below.)

You should have cut the trouser fronts with extensions of 4 cm (plus 1·5 cm seam allowance) beyond the centre-front (*Figure 79*).

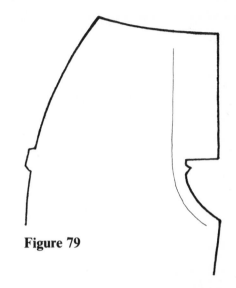

Figure 79

Left: *Concealed zip setting; right side*
Right: *Concealed zip setting; wrong side, showing zip-guard*

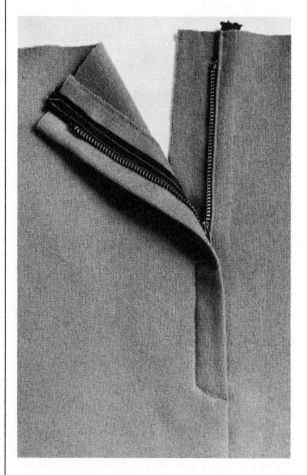

MAKING UP THE TROUSERS

1 Finish the edges of the extensions with zigzag stitching.

2 Mark with chalk the centre-front line of the left front, A–B in *Figure 80*.

3 Press back the left extension 1 cm beyond the centre-front line.

4 Pin the zip behind the fold, with the top of the chain a good 1·5 cm below the top edge of the fabric.

5 Cut a zip-guard the length of the extension and 6 cm wide. Finish its sides and lower end with zigzag stitching. Centre it behind the zip, and tack.

6 With a zipper foot, stitch close to the fold (*Figure 81*).

7 Turn to the wrong side and stitch together the turnings of trouser and guard, through the enclosed edge of the zipper tape.

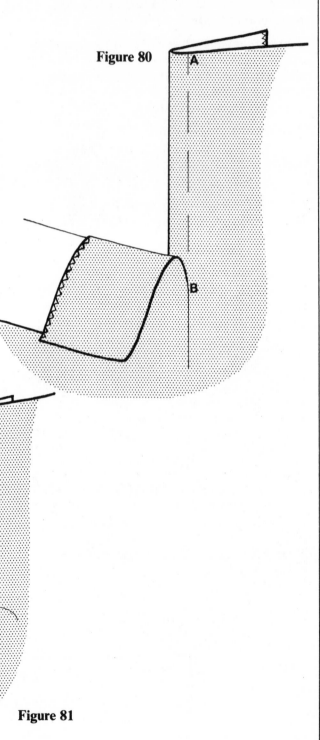

Figure 80

Figure 81

8 Pin the right front over the zip, matching the centre-front lines. Tack the folded edges together (*Figure 82*).

9 Fold the zip-guard out of the way. Tack and top-stitch the right-hand side of the opening, through the two thicknesses of fabric and the right zipper tape. Curve the stitching across below the end-stop of the zip.

10 Now, with the zip-guard folded back again to its proper place, stitch through all thicknesses to the seamline.

11 Through the right extension only, run a second row of machining down the right-hand zipper tape, for extra strength.

THE WAIST FINISH

The waistband
A straight waistband should be stiffened with iron-on interfacing, across half its width (not across the facing).

1 Trim off a scant 1 cm along the facing edge and finish it with zigzag stitching.

2 Stitch the short seams at each end of the waistband, stopping short of the seam allowance. Trim and turn the band right-side-out (*Figure 83*).

3 Make belt carriers by folding a strip of fabric in four (raw edges inside) and machining down each edge. Make them as one strip, then cut them into lengths. Stitch the belt-carriers in place, upside-down, at the fold line of the waistband. Press the carriers downwards; their lower ends are then taken into the waist seam.

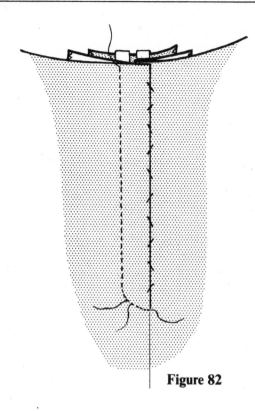

Figure 82

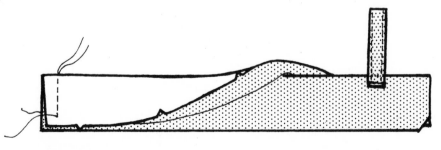

Figure 83

MAKING UP THE TROUSERS

4 With right sides together, match the waistband notches to the trouser seams, letting the extension come at the left-hand side of the trouser front, to correspond with the zip-guard if you have used one (*Figure 84*).

5 Stitch the waistline seam.

6 Press the turnings, and the ends of the zipper tapes, up inside the waistband. Tack the waistband facing in place, so that its zigzagged edge comes just below the seamline. From the right side, top-stitch exactly along the seamline to catch in the edge of the waistband facing. This stitching will sink invisibly into the seamline. *Figure 85* shows the right and wrong sides.

Shaped waistbands have a seam along their top edge. Interface the waistband; then with right sides together stitch it to its facing along the upper edge and ends (*Figure 86*). Trim, turn right-side-out and press. Continue as for straight waistbands.

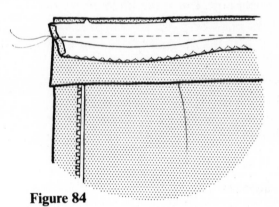

Figure 84

Figure 85

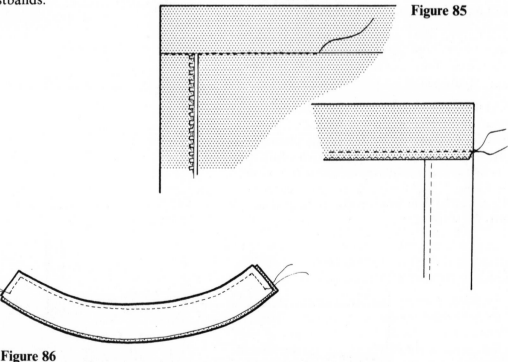

Figure 86

Petersham finish

Cut the petersham to the length of the waistline, plus a turning of 1 cm at each end.

With the petersham on the wrong side of the trousers, tack its edge to the waist seamline. From the wrong side, stitch close to this edge. *Figure 87* shows the right side.

Trim, and cover the raw edges with seam binding.

Fold the petersham to the inside of the trousers; attached in this way, no white edge of petersham can show along top of trousers.

Waistline hook and bar

With either waist finish, take the strain off the zip and make a firm waistline by using a heavy hook and bar (*Figure 88*).

Elasticated waistband

As there will be no front opening, first stitch the ends of the band together, leaving a gap on the facing side for threading in the elastic. Fold the waistband with right side outside, match both its edges to the trouser waistline, right sides together, and zigzag machine stitch all round. Trim the seam narrowly and finish the raw edges with zigzag machining.

HEM FINISHES

All finished hems should be pressed lightly at the fold. Do not press over the stitched edge of the hem, as it may leave a ridge mark on the right side. At this stage, give a final pressing also to the front and back trouser creases.

With binding

Use seam binding on straight-cut or tapered trouser hems. Machine one edge of the binding to the hem turning. Hem the other edge to the trouser leg (*Figure 89*).

On flared trousers use bias binding which will stretch round the curve of the hem. Open out one crease of the binding. Machine it along the crease to the hem turning. Fold upwards and slip-hem the other fold to the trouser leg (*Figure 90*).

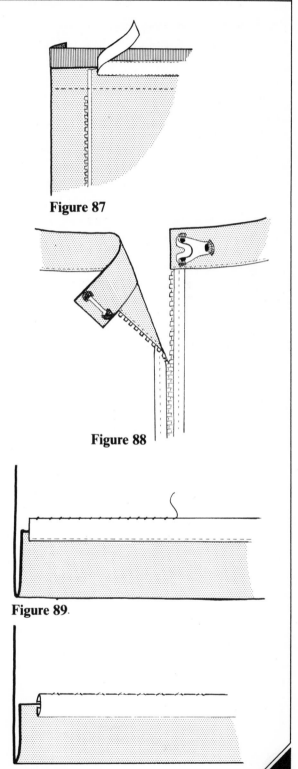

Figure 87

Figure 88

Figure 89.

Figure 90

With the blind-hemming stitch
This stitch is built into automatic and semi-automatic sewing machines (*Figure 91*).

1 Finish the edge of the hem turning with zigzag stitching.

2 Tack the hem turning in place (*Figure 92*).

3 Fold back the hem along the line of tacking (*Figure 93*).

4 Work the blind-hemming stitch on the edge of the turning. Let the straight stitches fall on the single thickness of fabric and the swing-stitch just bite into the fold. If you work too far from the fold the swing-stitch will miss it altogether; if you are too close to it, long vertical stitches will appear on the right side. It is worth trying this stitch on a scrap of fabric until you can judge the exact distance that will produce tiny inconspicuous stitches on the right side (*Figure 94*).

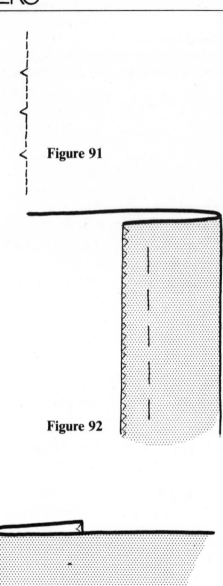

Figure 91

Figure 92

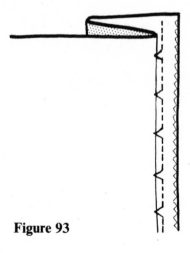

Figure 93

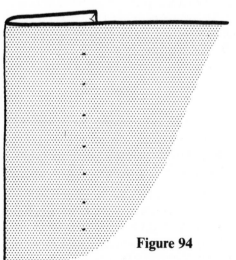

Figure 94

Trousers with turn-ups

Work the hem by one of the above methods.
Make the fold for the hem at the top of the
turn-up (A on *Figure 95*). Tack and press this
fold. The hem should be 7 cm deep from A
to B; 4 cm for the turn-up and 3 cm for the
hem itself. When finished, press the turn-ups
in place from the wrong side.

Trousers with elastic at the hem

Gathered trousers in very thin fabric can be
finished simply with a casing for elastic.

Turn up the 4 cm hem allowance, turn in the
top 1 cm and stitch along both folds (*Figure
96*).

Leave a 2 cm gap in the upper row of
stitching, for threading in the elastic.

Trousers with ankle bands

1 Make up the ankle bands, interfaced if
necessary, as shown in *Figure 97*. The two
layers of fabric are placed right sides together,
with the interfacing on top. Machine round
the three sides and the top edge of the
extension.

2 Trim and clip the seams, turn right-side-out
and press (*Figure 98*).

3 Unpick the bottom 7 cm on the leg side
seam.

4 Gather the trouser leg to fit the ankle band.

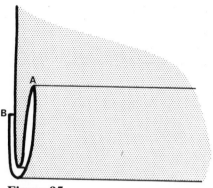

Figure 95

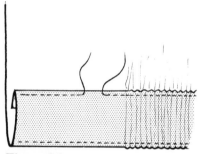

Figure 96

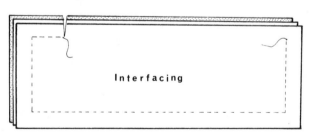

Interfacing

Figure 97

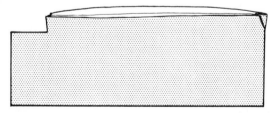

Figure 98

5 With right sides together, stitch the band and interfacing to the trousers. The underlap extension should be matched to the back of the opening (*Figure 99*).

6 On the wrong side, hem the band facing just below the machined seam (*Figure 100*). Finish with a pair of hooks and eyes.

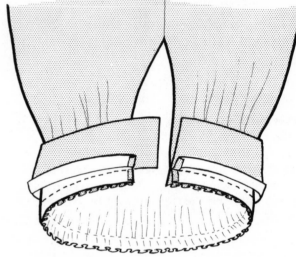

Figure 99

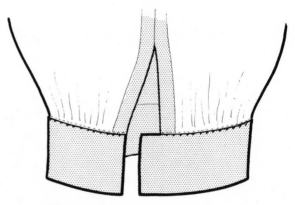

Figure 100